Bushbaby

Koala

Puppy

Kitten

Deer

Bear cub

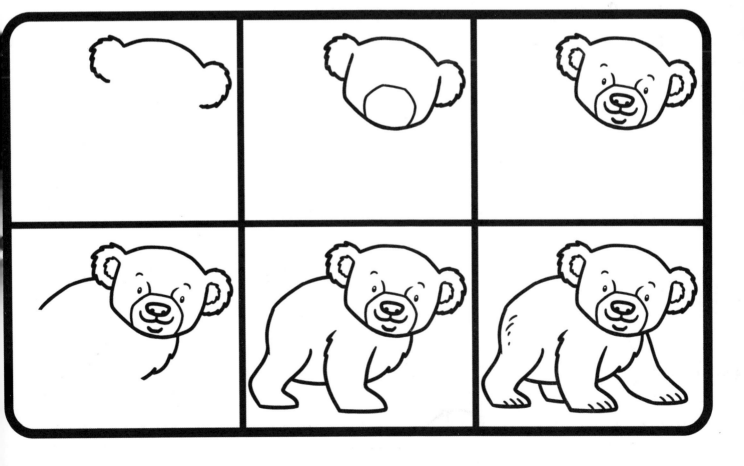

calf

foal

Piglet

Lion cub

Dolphin

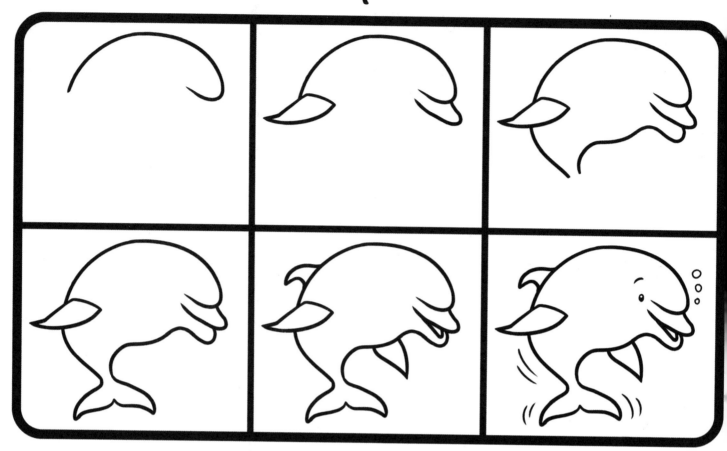

Duckling

Elephant

Fox cub

Kid

Hedgehog

Gibbon

Bat

Armadillo

Hippo

Joey

Mouse

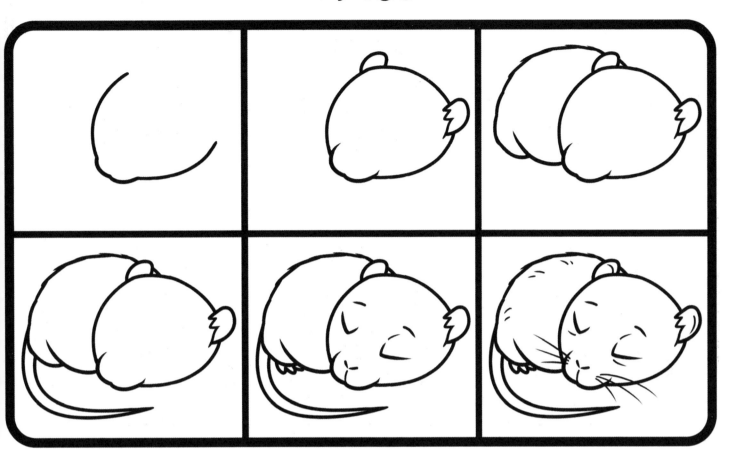

owlet

Panda

Penguin chick

Meerkat

Rhino

Seal Pup

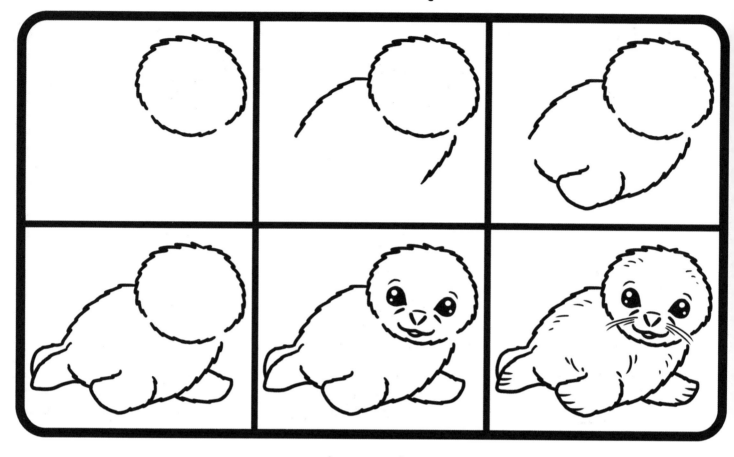

Lamb

cygnet

Turtle

Wolf Pup

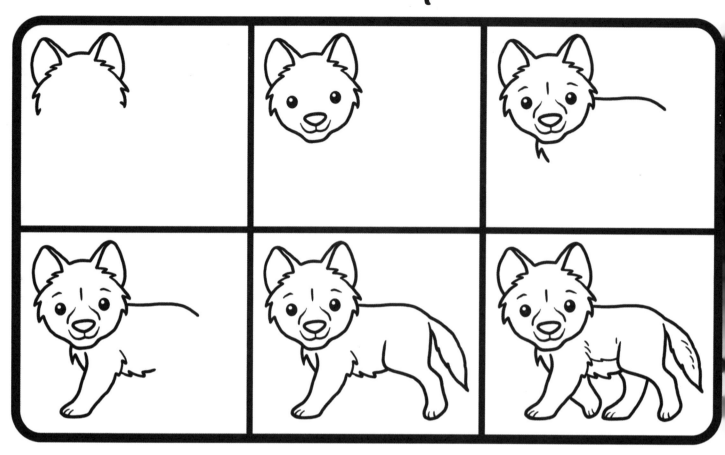

Zebra

Chimpanzee

Lemur

Cassowary

Baboon

Gerbil

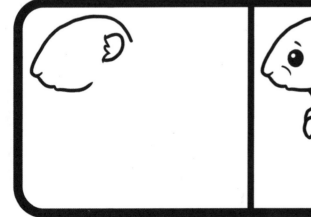

orangutan

Gorilla

Blue Whale

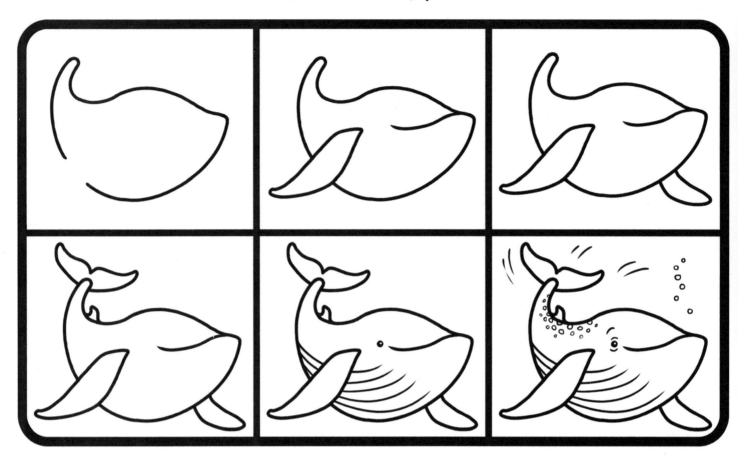

Polar Bear cub

orca

otter

Leopard cub

Cheetah cub

fennec fox

Tiger cub

Snow Leopard Cub

Sea Lion Pup

Manatee

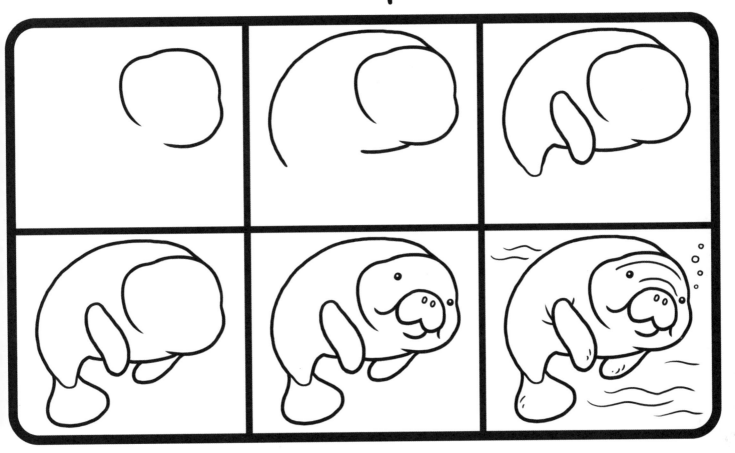

Giraffe

American Bison

Wildebeest

Howler Monkey

Possum

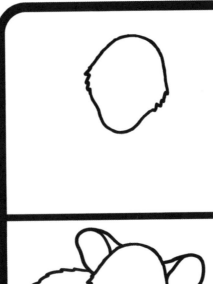

Dik-dik

flamingo

Bald Eagle

Donkey

Toucan

Tortoise

Chameleon

crocodile

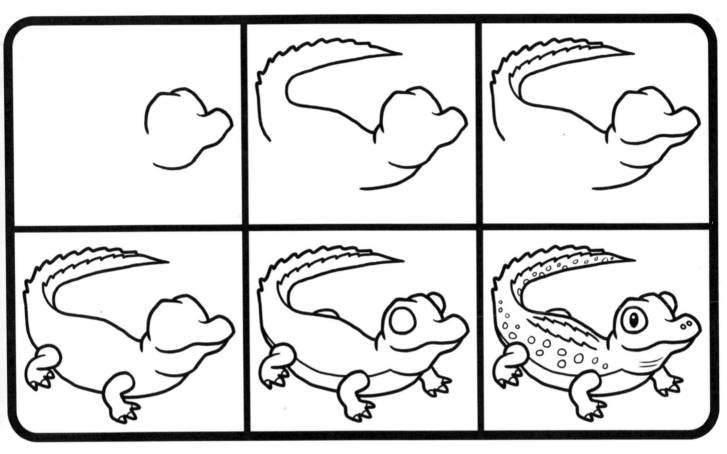

Rabbit

Whale Shark

Squirrel

Badger

Elephant Shrew

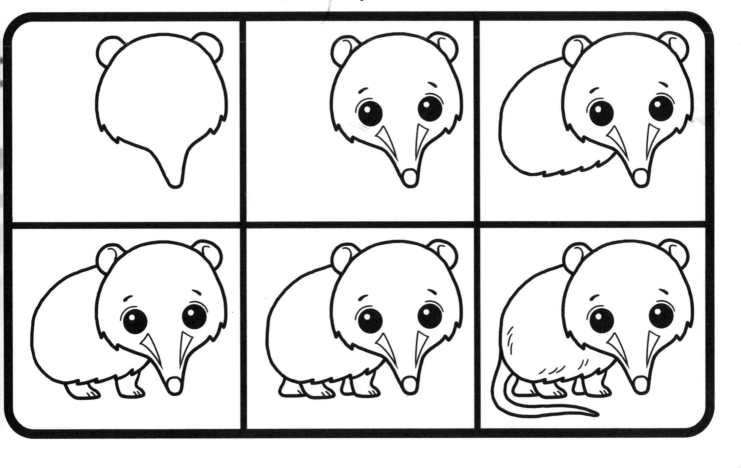

Weasel

Pelican

Tapir

ostrich

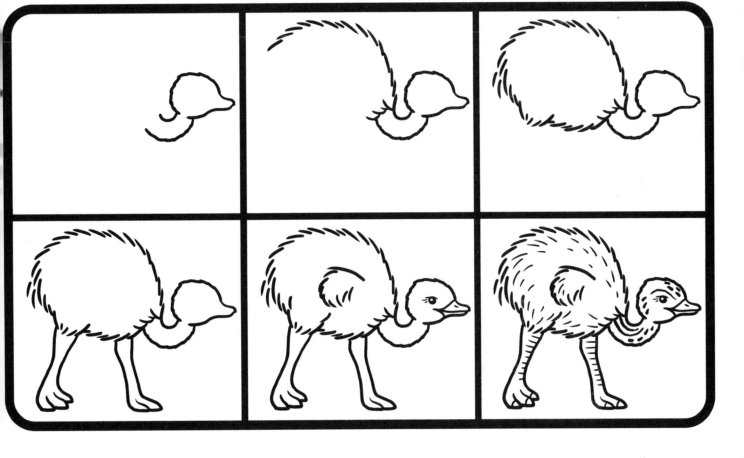

Heron

Lynx cub

Spider Monkey

Wombat Baby

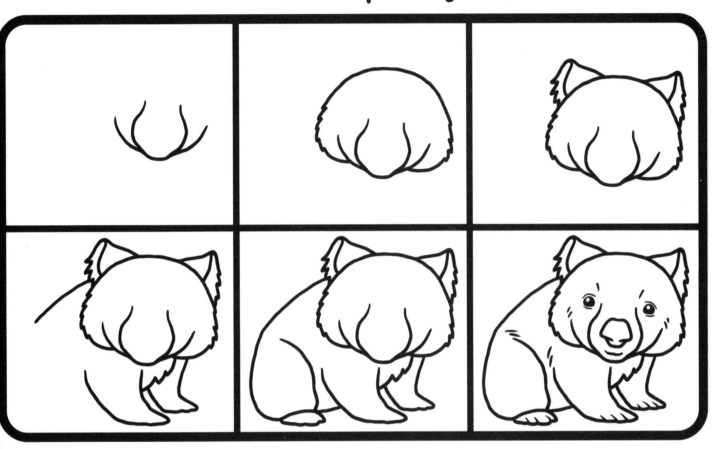

Thomson's Gazelle

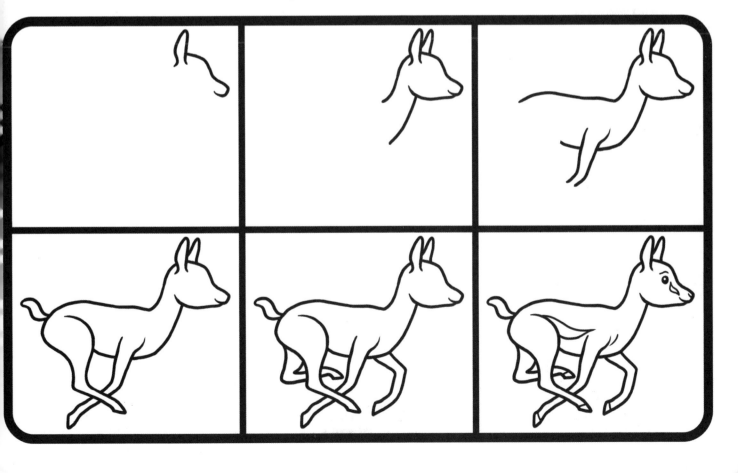

Beaver

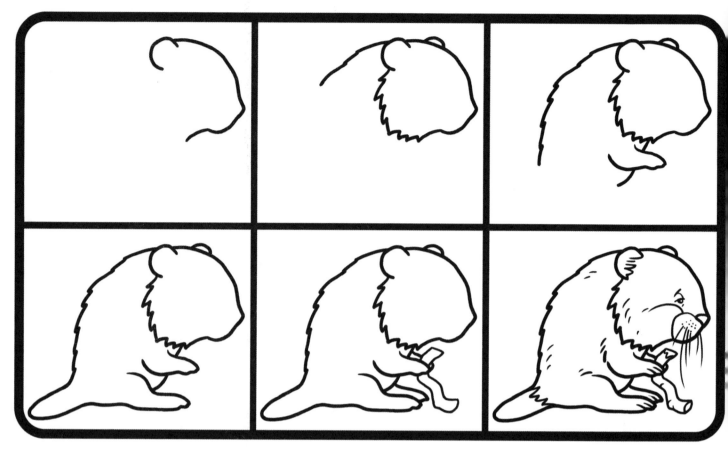

Skunk

Llama

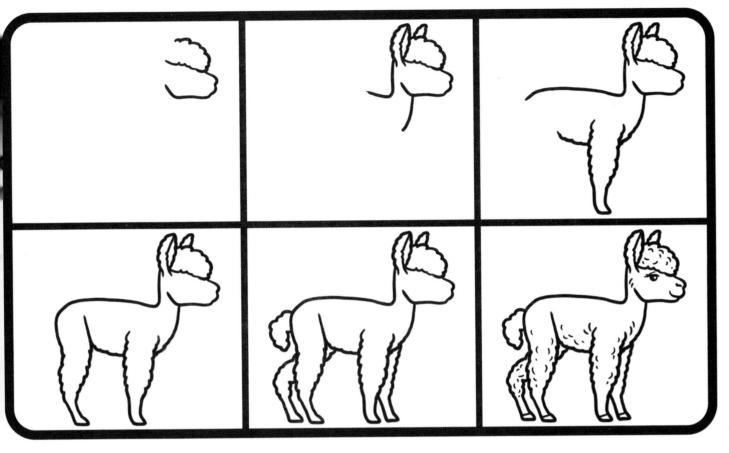

Dromedary camel

Warthog

Aardvark

Puma cub

Marmoset

Hyena cub

Mara

Raccoon

Sloth

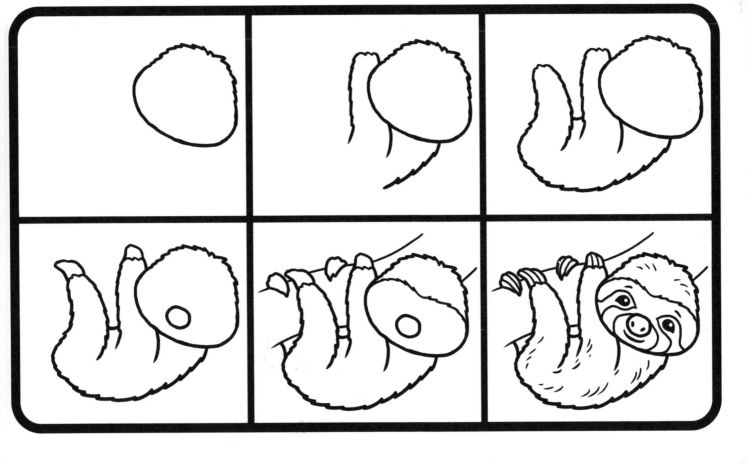

Mongoose

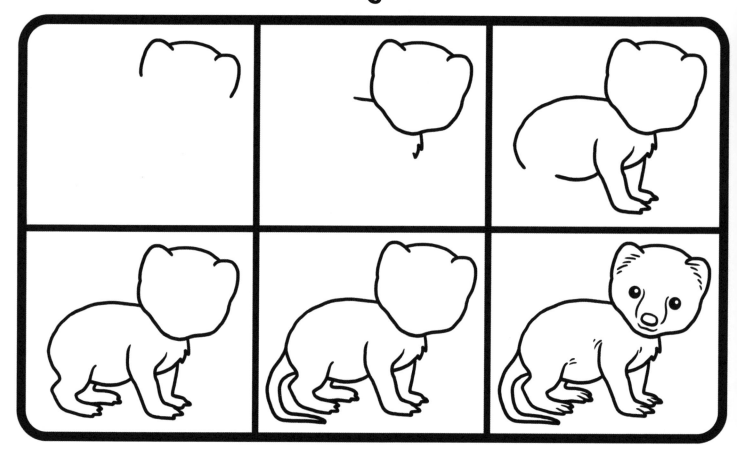

Shark

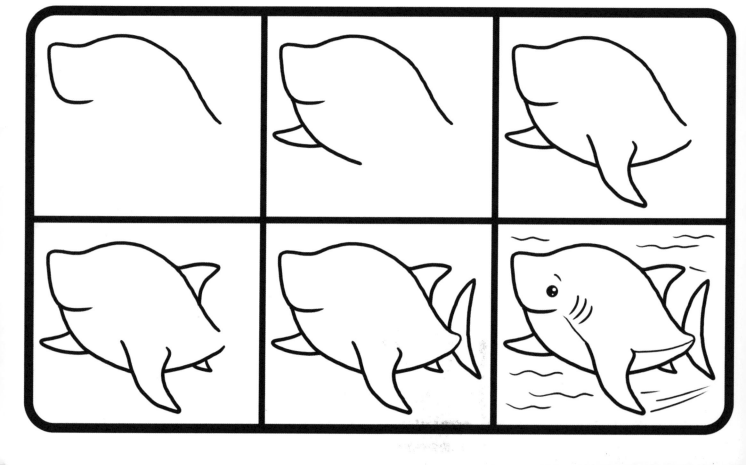

Loris

Mandrill

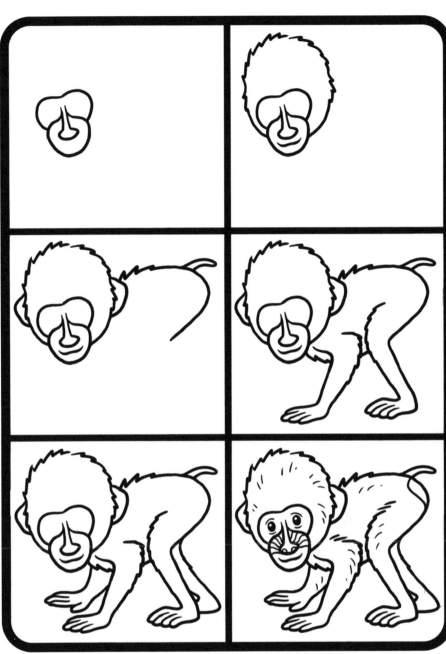

Platypus

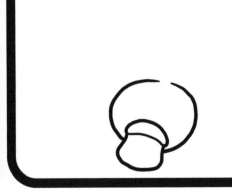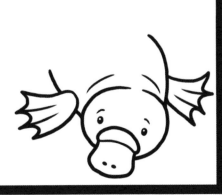

Guinea Pig

Chinchilla

Porcupine

Moose

Woodchuck

Arctic Hare